IT'S MY STATE!

NEW MEXICO

Ruth Bjorklund

Ellen H. Todras

Cavendish Square

New York

Published in 2014 by Cavendish Square Publishing, LLC
303 Park Avenue South, Suite 1247, New York, NY 10010

Library of Congress Cataloging-in-Publication Data
Bjorklund, Ruth.
        New Mexico / Ruth Bjorklund and Ellen H. Todras.—2nd ed.
            p. cm.—(It's my state!)
        Includes bibliographical references and index.
        Summary: "Surveys the history, geography, government, economy, and people of New Mexico"—Provided by publisher.
        ISBN 978-1-60870-882-6 (hardcover)—ISBN 978-1-62712-095-1 (paperback)—ISBN 978-1-60870-888-8 (ebook)
        1. New Mexico—Juvenile literature. 2. New Mexico—Social life and customs—Juvenile literature. I. Todras, Ellen H., 1947- II. Title.
    F796.3.B56 2013
    978.9—dc23   2012005175

This edition developed for Cavendish Square Publishing by RJF Publishing LLC (www.RJFpublishing.com))
Series Designer, Second Edition: Tammy West/Westgraphix LLC

All maps, illustrations, and graphics © Cavendish Square Publishing, LLC. Maps and artwork on pages 6, 40, 41, 76, and back cover by Christopher Santoro. Map and graphics on pages 11 and 44 by Westgraphix LLC.

The photographs in this book are used by permission and through the courtesy of:
Front cover: John Warden/Superstock and Robert Harding Picture Library/Superstock (inset).
Alamy: Andrew Holt, 5 (right); Andrea Pistolesi, 8; George H.H. Huey, 10; tbkmedia.de, 13 (bottom); Chris Howes, 22 (right); North Wind Picture Archives, 25, 27, 28; ClassicStock, 38; Chuck Place, 39; Picture Press Ltd., 46 (left); dieKlienert, 46 (right); David South, 48; Kalle Pahajoki, 49; M L Pearson, 50; Zuma Press, Inc., 56; PJF News, 64. **Associated Press:** Associated Press, 30, 32, 58, 60, 69 (top). **Corbis:** CORBIS, 31; Catherine Karnow, 53 (top); Robert E. Rosales/ZUMA Press, 59; Richard T. Nowitz, 68, 72. **Getty Images:** MPI, 29; WireImages, 47; Getty Images, 52. **North Wind Picture Archives:** North Wind Picture Archives, 20, 42; Nancy Carter/North Wind Picture Archives, 22 (left). **Superstock:** age fotostock, 4 (left), 4 (right), 44, 54; Glow Images, 5 (left); Exactostock, 9; Prisma, 12, 23; John Warden, 13 (top); Ray Laskowitz, 14; Ernest Manewal, 15; James Urbach, 16; Minden Pictures, 17, 34; Robert Harding Picture Library, 18 (left); Animals Animals, 18 (right); Wolfgang Kaehler, 19 (left); Nomad, 19 (right); Photri Inc./age fotostock, 26; Photri Images, 33; Stock Connection, 36, 45, 62; SuperStock, 43; J Burke Photography, 51; Steve Vidler, 53 (bottom), 65; SOMOS, 67; BSIP, 70; Flirt, 71 (left); Chris Selby/age fotostock, 71 (right); Visions of America, 73. **www.rgbphoto.com:** 69 (bottom).

Printed in the United States of America

NEW MEXICO

CONTENTS

State Flower: Yucca

The yucca is a spiky plant that can grow as tall as 30 feet (9 meters). It has white flowers on the end of its long slender stalk. Early settlers used the roots to make soap. The leaves were used to make rope and twine.

State Tree: Piñon Pine

Piñon (PEEN-yon) pines grow slowly, but they can reach heights of up to 35 feet (11 m). The depth of the root system below ground can be equal to the tree's height. The piñon is prized for the sweet smell of its wood and for its tasty seed, the pine nut.

State Bird: Greater Roadrunner

Also known as the chaparral bird, the greater roadrunner is a desert bird that feeds on insects, lizards, and snakes. It would rather run or walk than fly. Able to race at speeds up to 15 miles (24 kilometers) per hour, the roadrunner is quick enough to chase and devour a rattlesnake.

State Gem: Turquoise

The gemstone turquoise has copper, iron, and a green mineral called variscite in it. These give turquoise its color, which makes it both valuable and beautiful. The Navajo and Pueblo Indians have been mining turquoise for ornamental use for hundreds of years. Making jewelry using turquoise set in silver is a big industry in New Mexico today.

State Vegetables: Frijoles and Chiles

The New Mexico legislature declared frijoles (free-HO-lays) and chiles the state vegetables in 1965. The Pueblo Indians began growing frijoles, or pinto beans, centuries ago. In the 1500s, Spanish settlers brought chiles (spicy red or green peppers) to New Mexico from Mexico. The two vegetables have been key ingredients in the area's diet ever since.

State Fossil: *Coelophysis*

Coelophysis (see-loh-FIE-sis) was a small dinosaur that lived on Earth about 228 million years ago. This meat-eating dinosaur was about 9 feet (2.7 m) long, with a pointed head, jagged teeth, and three claws on each hand. Its name means "hollow form," because its bones were hollow. Scientists discovered hundreds of *Coelophysis* skeletons in a bone bed near Ghost Ranch, New Mexico, in the 1940s.

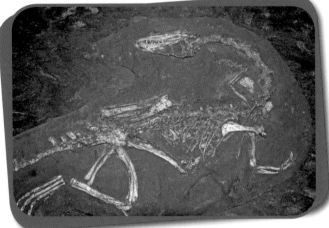

Land of Enchantment

New Mexico is a land of natural wonders. From soaring mountains to deep, dark caves, from vast golden deserts to red canyon walls, the land glows under dazzling skies. Author Charles Lummis has written, "Most of New Mexico, most of the year, is a . . . harmony of browns and grays, over which the enchanted light of its blue skies casts an eternal spell. . . ." Visitors and residents alike can see why New Mexico is called the "Land of Enchantment."

The state is divided into thirty-three counties. Although New Mexicans love the natural beauty of the state's landscapes, today about two-thirds of them live in urban areas. Albuquerque is the state's largest city, with more than 545,000 residents. Santa Fe, the state capital, has a population of about 68,000.

The Landscape

New Mexico ranks thirty-sixth among all U.S. states in terms of population, but it is the nation's fifth-largest state in terms of size. Its land area is 121,298 square miles (314,160 square kilometers), barely enough to hold all of the state's variety.

New Mexico's landscape is extraordinary. The majestic Rocky Mountains tower over the northern

Quick Facts

NEW MEXICO BORDERS

North	Colorado
South	Texas
	Mexico
East	Oklahoma
	Texas
West	Arizona
Northwest	Utah

Enchanted Mesa in west-central New Mexico rises more than 400 feet (120 m) above the surrounding land.

part of the state, while the vast prairies of the Great Plains cover eastern New Mexico. The mighty Rio Grande (Spanish for "big river") flows north to south through the center of the state. In other parts of New Mexico, there are more mountain ranges, mesas (broad, flat-topped hills with cliff-like sides), canyons, valleys, caverns, rivers, and arroyos (dry riverbeds that fill with water when it rains or when snow melts).

The Rocky Mountains and the Great Plains

The southern end of the Rocky Mountains covers northern New Mexico. The

Quick Facts

FOUR CORNERS
The area known as the Four Corners is the place where Colorado, Utah, Arizona, and New Mexico meet. Each state is one corner. This is the only place in the United States where four states come together.

Rio Grande flows through the southern Rockies and splits it into ranges that have been given their own names. One of these ranges is the Sangre de Cristo Mountains. This is where snow-covered Wheeler Peak rises. At 13,161 feet (4,011 m), it is the tallest point in the state. The landscape in New Mexico's mountains includes canyons, ancient lava flows, and high mountain meadows. Nearby, there are cities and towns such as Los Alamos, Taos, and Santa Fe.

Grasslands cover New Mexico's Great Plains region. Short, hardy bunchgrasses such as blue grama and buffalo grass grow as far as the eye can see. The southeastern section is called "El Llano Estacado," which means "staked plains" in Spanish. Some say the term comes from Spanish explorers who long ago pounded stakes into the ground to mark their routes. With an average of seventeen people per square mile, it is a remote land of open spaces and vast ranches.

More than a hundred years ago, ranchers began raising cattle in this area. The cattle stripped the prairie of its grasses. In times of drought, the grass would not grow, cattle could not eat, and ranches failed. In some parts of the region farmers plowed the land to grow crops, but many farms also failed in times of drought. In what is now New Mexico's Kiowa National Grassland, the U.S. government bought ranches and farms, and it tried to replant the prairie.

The Sangre de Cristo Mountains include dozens of peaks that are more than 13,000 feet (4,000 m) high.

In the Kiowa National Grassland in northeastern New Mexico, the federal government has tried to restore the area's natural prairie.

The grass did not grow as well, so government officials turned to a biologist named Allan Savory. Savory said that, historically, healthy prairie needed bison (also called buffalo). He noted that when wild bison fed on prairie grass, they stayed in herds, ate the grass to the ground, and stomped on what they did not eat. The trampled grass turned into sod, a rich soil in which new grass could grow. Cattle do not usually graze in the same way as wild buffalo. So Savory suggested that cattle should be fenced together to graze on the land, so that they too could trample the prairie grass. It worked. Native grasses and wildflowers that had not bloomed in decades now flourish in the Kiowa National Grassland.

In Their Own Words

New Mexico . . . was great, and splendid. . . . The landscape lived, and lived as the world of the gods.

—English novelist D. H. Lawrence

The Intermountain Region

The intermountain region covers southern, central, and western New Mexico. The area has several ranges, including the Zuni, Mogollon, Cibola, Sandia, Guadalupe, and San Andres Mountains. Many of these

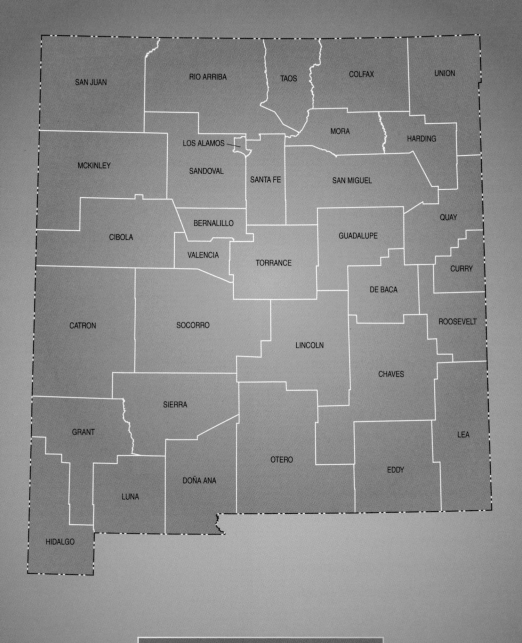

New Mexico has 33 counties.

ranges are named after American Indian tribes. The Rio Grande brings life-giving water from the Rocky Mountains all the way to the Mexican border. Other rivers, such as the San Juan, the Gila (HEE-la), and the Pecos, nourish a variety of plant and animal life. In other parts of the region, there are high mesas, caves, canyons, and badlands (areas with large rock formations and very little plant life).

Near the Pecos River in southern New Mexico is Carlsbad Caverns, one of the most famous cave systems in the world. Its Big Room is the largest underground chamber in North America. Visitors who stay until sunset can watch hundreds of thousands of Mexican free-tailed bats stream out of the caves. Scientists say the bats can eat 11 tons (10 metric tons) of insects on a summer night.

Another natural wonder in New Mexico is the 275 square miles (712 sq km) of dunes in the southern part of the state now protected as part of the White Sands National Monument. Billions of tons of a white mineral called selenite, or gypsum, form these dunes, which are mounds of sand that pile up when the winds blow.

Western New Mexico has many wilderness areas. The country's first national wilderness is among them. The Gila Wilderness, part of the Gila National Forest, is where ancient people once lived in cliff dwellings. It is also a land of dry mesas, steep canyons, and badlands. From the rock formations called the Bisti Badlands in the northwestern corner of the state, you can travel 700-year-old roads into Chaco Canyon. There, ancient people built a huge city in the canyon walls.

As it flows south, the Rio Grande passes through gorges in New Mexico that are up to 800 feet (245 m) deep.

Visitors to the Chaco Culture National Historical Park can still see the remains of this amazing accomplishment.

The Climate

The climate of New Mexico is generally mild, sunny, and dry. The average rainfall is about 13 inches (33 centimeters) per year. Winters are drier than summers. Temperatures and precipitation (the amount of water an area receives in the form of rain, snow, sleet, and hail) can vary widely from day to night, from summer to winter, from mountain to valley, and from north to south. The south gets about 8 inches (20 cm) of rainfall each year. But in the north, the total is closer to 30 inches (76 cm).

The effects of weather over thousands of years have created fascinating rock formations in the Bisti Badlands.

Quick Facts

NEW MEXICO'S WORLD HERITAGE SITES

World Heritage Sites are special cultural or natural sites chosen by the United Nations. These sites are considered among the most important in the entire world. The Great Wall of China and the pyramids of Egypt are some examples. New Mexico has three World Heritage Sites: Carlsbad Caverns (right), Chaco Canyon, and the Taos Pueblo.

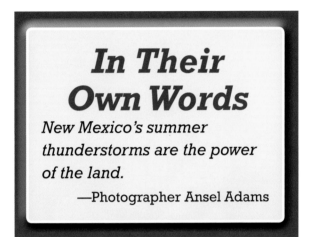
In winter, cold air moves south from Canada and brings snow to the mountains, as well as occasional snow to the valleys. Year-round average temperatures are 50 to 60 degrees Fahrenheit (10 to 16 degrees Celsius). But temperatures can rise to 100 °F (38 °C) in the summer and fall below 0 °F (−18 °C) in the winter.

Artist Georgia O'Keeffe, who spent many years in New Mexico, wrote that the area is "more sky than earth." During the summer months, brief, heavy thunderstorms are common. New Mexico

Impressive storm clouds can bring heavy rain showers and lightning strikes in the summer months.

has more lightning strikes than any other state. As one resident has said, "The lightning is absolutely terrifying; it's so right there in front of you. We just stay inside until it's over." When thunderclouds pour rain, the arroyos fill quickly and often create dangerous flash floods. But in dry regions, the thunderclouds bring more wind than rain, stirring the dust into tornado-like swirls called dust devils.

Wildlife

Many different types of plants and animals can be found throughout New Mexico. The forests in the mountain regions are lush with pine, fir, aspen, and spruce trees. Clear streams and lakes are filled with Rio Grande trout. Roaming freely in the high country are elk, mule deer, bobcats, and mountain lions. Coyotes, bighorn sheep, and bears inhabit the land as well. The American black bear is the official state mammal. Black bears roam the state's woodlands, eating berries, nuts, fruits, and other plants, as well as rodents and other small animals. They have coats that can be either brown or black, and they can weigh from 200 to 600 pounds (from 90 to 270 kilograms).

New Mexico's deserts and canyons are filled with cactuses and other plants that thrive in the hot and dry conditions. Lizards, snakes, spiders, scorpions, and small rodents scamper across the dusty ground. In the sky, eagles and hawks soar in search of prey. The climate presents a challenge to some nesting desert birds. They do not always sit on their eggs to keep them warm. Sometimes they will spread their wings above their nest to block the sun and keep the eggs cool.

A study by the U.S. government concluded that about 6,000 black bears were living in New Mexico in the early twenty-first century.

Sandhill cranes may travel from as far north as Canada to spend the winter in New Mexico.

Along the Rio Grande, in the Bosque del Apache National Wildlife Refuge, hundreds of thousands of birds gather. Many types of birds that spend the summer farther north fly south to Bosque del Apache for the winter. Visitors to the refuge can see tropical songbirds, raptors (birds of prey), ducks, geese, and giant sandhill cranes. Lucky bird-watchers may even catch a glimpse of endangered species, such as the American whooping crane. When a species (a type of animal or plant) is endangered, there are so few left that the species is at risk of becoming extinct, or completely dying out.

Endangered Wildlife in New Mexico

New Mexico's plants and animals are an important part of the state. Many residents try to help the state's wildlife in a number of ways. They conserve scarce resources such as water, protect the natural habitats of plants and animals and make sure that threatened or endangered animals are not hunted. A species is considered threatened when its numbers are reduced and it is at risk of becoming endangered. There are 122 species of threatened or endangered animals in New Mexico. These include the Chiricahua leopard frog, the New Mexican ridge-nosed rattlesnake, Baird's sparrow, and the white-sided jackrabbit.

The U.S. Fish and Wildlife Service has been working to restore the populations of some endangered species in New Mexico. For example, the Mexican gray wolf was nearly extinct by the 1970s. The Fish and Wildlife Service began to breed the wolves in captivity. In 1998, the service began releasing these wolves into the wild. Although the Mexican gray wolf remains endangered, its population is increasing.

The smallest of the five types of gray wolves, the Mexican gray wolf is about the size of a German shepherd dog.

Plants & Animals

Century Plant

The century plant is just one of the many kinds of agave plants native to New Mexico. For its first five to thirty-five years, the century plant grows a clump of tough, stiff leaves that store food and water. Then, using the stored nutrients, a flower stalk appears. It grows as quickly as a foot (0.3 m) per day and can reach a height of 15 feet (5 m). Large tubular flowers bloom along the stalk, giving off scents that attract insects and bats. Soon after flowering, though, the plant dies. American Indians roasted and ate the stalks and used them to make flutes. The century plant was also used in making rope, rugs, baskets, and cloth.

Javelina

The javelina, or collared peccary, is the only native wild boar in the United States. Javelinas have large heads with piglike snouts, slender legs, and sharp, straight tusks. Their name comes from the Spanish *javelina*, which means "javelin" or "spear." The animals feed at dawn and at dusk and are fond of prickly pear cactus.

American Pika

The American pika, also known as the cony or rock rabbit, is part of the hare and rabbit family of animals. It looks like a guinea pig. The pika lives in high, rocky places and is known for its squeaking sounds. When no other animals are around, the pika dashes from its den and grabs mouthfuls of grass. It lays the grass in the sun, building little haystacks, and stores the dried grass for its winter diet.

Prickly Pear Cactus

The prickly pear cactus has sharp yellow or red spines all over its flat, fleshy pads, which look like leaves but are actually branches. Many desert animals seek the prickly pear for the water in its pads. Some people cut off the spines and prepare the pads as a vegetable called *nopalitos*.

Turkey Vulture

The turkey vulture soars overhead looking for animals that have recently died. Its Latin name (*Cathartes aura*) means "purifier" because the vultures rid the countryside of decaying animals. The turkey vulture is brown with a red, featherless head that resembles a turkey's. Unlike other birds, turkey vultures have a strong sense of smell. In some cases, engineers have used turkey vultures to sniff out gas leaks in pipelines.

Western Banded Gecko

At night, this desert lizard hunts for insects, spiders, and baby scorpions. After a good meal, the gecko cleans its face with its tongue. It stores extra food as fat in its tail. If a predator should step on that tail, it will snap off. But the banded gecko can grow a new one.

From the Beginning

Long before Europeans set sail for North America, great cultures thrived in the land that is now called New Mexico. In spite of the region's rugged landscape, early peoples in the area lived in harmony with the land, just as present-day New Mexicans live in harmony with the ways of the past.

The Old Ones

Around 12,000 years ago, New Mexico's first people roamed the grasslands hunting bison, mammoths, mastodons, and antelope. They made tools and weapons out of stone and bone. Eventually, the climate became drier, and many types of large animals died out or migrated to other areas in search of food. So the people—ancestors of today's American Indians—started a new way of life. They hunted smaller animals and gathered nuts and berries. After a time, they built villages out of dried mud and stone, and they began growing crops such as corn, squash, melons, and beans.

Two of these ancient groups were the Mogollon in what is now southwestern New Mexico and the Ancestral Puebloans in the north. (The Ancestral Puebloans are sometimes referred to as the Anasazi.) The first pottery in the Southwest was made by the Mogollon. They also built round houses that were set partly below ground. The houses faced a central plaza. Each village also included a kiva. A kiva is a circular room with a central fireplace used by men and boys for worship or

Navajo people have lived in New Mexico
for hundreds of years.

rituals. Usually made of adobe—sun-dried bricks formed from clay, water, and straw or grass—it often can be entered only by a ladder through a hole in the roof. Kivas still exist in ancient ruins throughout New Mexico and are found in many present-day American Indian villages as well.

The Mogollon were expert farmers. They traded with the other ancient group, the Ancestral Puebloans. The Ancestral Puebloans were mainly basket makers and hunters and gatherers. But they soon learned farming and pottery making from the Mogollon. The Ancestral Puebloans used stone and adobe to build extraordinary towns, plazas, kivas, and cliff dwellings. Their largest city was in Chaco Canyon. Chaco was an important site for trading, as well as a cultural and religious center. Hundreds of hand-laid stone roads lead into Chaco. Small bands of Ancestral Puebloan families built houses that can still be seen along these roads. These simple villages are called "Chaco outliers." As a Taos photographer has said, "Chaco is simply magical."

The Mogollon people created many petroglyphs, which are pictures or symbols carved into a rock surface. At Gila Cliff Dwellings National Monument, visitors can see the remains of an ancient Mogollon village.

CHACO CULTURE NATIONAL HISTORICAL PARK

In addition to being a World Heritage Site, Chaco Canyon is a national historical park, managed by the U.S. National Park Service. There are thirteen major ruins and more than 400 smaller archaeological sites in the park.

By around 1300–1400, the Ancestral Puebloan and Mogollon civilizations had mysteriously disappeared. Many scientists believe these ancestor tribes left their villages because water became scarce. They probably joined with other native cultures. Today's Pueblo Indian people, who had established a number of villages in the region by the 1500s, are believed to be their descendants.

Other native groups, such as the Navajo and the Apache, moved south from areas in present-day Canada to what is now New Mexico. In the beginning, these tribes were nomadic. This means that they moved from place to place, following bison herds and hunting for food. When hunting became harder because there were fewer bison, the Navajo and the Apache raided Pueblo villages for food and other supplies. Eventually, the nomadic tribes settled into their own villages and began farming. Today, the country's largest Indian reservation, the Navajo Nation, covers part of northwestern New Mexico, as well as parts of Arizona and Utah.

NAMES FOR THE NAVAJO

The name *Navajo* comes from a word used by other tribes to describe where the Navajo lived. It means "large planted fields." In their own language, the Navajo call themselves Diné (Dee-NAY), meaning "the people."

The Spanish Enter

Not long after the Navajo and Apache moved into present-day New Mexico, Spanish explorers arrived in the region. They had conquered the native peoples of Mexico and made the area into a Spanish colony. The Spanish then moved north, searching for gold, silver, gems, and other treasures to send to the king of Spain.

The first Spaniard who may have set foot in what is now New Mexico was Álvar Núñez Cabeza de Vaca in 1536. He and three companions had been part of a shipwrecked expedition that landed in western Florida in 1528. The men spent several years as slaves to American Indians in what is now Texas. They heard stories from the native people about the Seven Cities of Cíbola, which were cities thought to be so rich that the streets were lined with gold. After escaping from his captors, Cabeza de Vaca made his way through the Southwest and down to Mexico by 1536, and he related these stories to others. Francisco Vásquez de Coronado, starting from Mexico in 1540, ventured hundreds of miles into the Great Plains in search of the Seven Cities of Cíbola. He did not find them (they did not exist) and reported to the king of Spain, "[It] troubled me greatly to find myself on these limitless plains, where I was in great need of water, and often had to drink it so poor that it was more mud than water." But the lure of riches sent more Spaniards north from Mexico on El Camino Real, "the royal road," into the land they called New Mexico. As Spanish soldiers, settlers, explorers, and priests came upon native villages with buildings made of mud, they called them pueblos after the Spanish word for "town." The Indians living in these villages also became known as Pueblos.

The Spanish had two reasons for exploring the region. One was finding treasure, and the other was spreading the Roman Catholic faith. At first, the native people were friendly toward the newcomers, but the Spanish proved to be terrifying. The Indians had never seen men on horseback. Some were frightened by the gleaming swords the Spanish carried as weapons and by the violence of the newcomers.

The first Spanish settlement in New Mexico was near the Rio Grande, north of present-day Santa Fe. In 1598, four hundred settlers led by Don Juan de

Oñate established haciendas, or ranches. The settlers found it difficult to farm the dry land and forced the Indians to work the fields. Oñate built Catholic missions throughout the region, and priests tried to make the Indians practice Christianity. The Spanish burned kivas, destroyed sacred objects, and challenged Indian religious leaders. Oñate's soldiers were so brutal that he was eventually sent back to Mexico City in disgrace. Spain wanted to abandon New Mexico completely, but the priests refused to leave behind the Indians who had become Christians. So Spain declared that New Mexico would be missionary land.

Quick Facts

SPANISH NAMES OF PUEBLO VILLAGES

When the Spanish came across a Pueblo village, they assigned it a patron saint. Today, there are nineteen traditional Pueblo villages in New Mexico. Some of them have kept their Spanish saint names, such as Santa Clara, San Felipe, San Juan, Santa Ana, and San Ildefonso.

Then, in 1609, a new Spanish governor arrived, Don Pedro de Peralta. He established a new capital city and named it Santa Fe. Despite the new leader,

After being shipwrecked in Florida in 1528, Álvar Núñez Cabeza de Vaca made his way to the Spanish colony of Mexico over a period of eight years.

Salinas Pueblo Missions National Monument includes the ruins of four Spanish mission churches built in the 1600s.

the relationship between the Spanish and the American Indians did not improve. The Indians resented working on the haciendas, tending the mission gardens, wearing European clothing, and being forced to accept a religion other than their own.

By 1680, the Pueblo people had had enough. A religious leader named Popé led the most successful revolt by native peoples in the New World, an event that became known as the Pueblo Revolt. Pueblo leaders sent runners as messengers to the many Indian communities to inform them of the planned revolt. Every community leader received a knotted rope. Each day, the leaders untied a knot. When all the knots were gone, the Indians knew it was time to fight. They surrounded the Spanish settlements and forced the Spanish to withdraw. Although the Spanish returned in 1692, led by Don Diego de Vargas, they allowed the Pueblos to practice their ancestral religion along with Christianity. For more than a hundred years after the Pueblo Indians' victory, Spain continued to control New Mexico.

Mexican Province and U.S. Territory

When Mexico gained its independence from Spain in 1821, New Mexico became a province of Mexico. The Mexican rulers were much more interested in trade with the United States than the Spanish had been. American traders established the Santa Fe Trail. It ran from Missouri to Santa Fe and brought many trade goods to New Mexico. These included clothing, candles, books, furniture, and knives. In exchange, New Mexicans sent furs and silver eastward on the trail.

Covered wagons carried trade goods to and from New Mexico along the Santa Fe Trail. This illustration shows a wagon train entering the town of Santa Fe at the end of its journey.

In 1846, the United States declared war on Mexico. A U.S. general named Stephen Kearny led his troops into New Mexico and took over the province. Two years later, the United States and Mexico signed a treaty that made most of present-day New Mexico part of the United States. (In the Gadsden Purchase of 1853, the United States bought from Mexico an additional strip of land in what is now southern New Mexico and Arizona.)

In 1850, Congress established the Territory of New Mexico. The region had a territorial government but was not yet a state. When the Civil War began in 1861, both the Union and the Confederate governments wanted New Mexico on their side. Union and Confederate forces met and fought in New Mexico in 1862, at the Battle of Glorieta Pass. The Union victory in that battle essentially ended any Confederate threat to U.S. control of New Mexico.

In the mid–1800s, Americans of northern European descent, known as Anglo Americans or Anglos, moved into New Mexico. They came to find new homes,

After New Mexico became part of the United States, cattle ranching became more important. Anglos, Hispanics, and American Indians all worked as cowboys.

By the late 1800s, most of New Mexico's American Indians had been forced onto reservations. This general store was on an Apache reservation, just south of the present-day city of Ruidoso.

adventure, and gold. Warrior tribes, such as the Apache, Comanche, Kiowa, and Navajo had bitter feelings about the Anglos invading their lands. Bloody fighting took place over several decades between U.S. soldiers and American Indians, including Apache groups led by warriors such as Geronimo and Cochise. In the 1860s, the U.S. government sent Kit Carson to round up Navajo groups and force them onto a reservation in eastern New Mexico. Carson was a trapper and a scout who had friends among the Indian tribes. Still, he followed government orders and in 1864 forced thousands of Navajos to walk 300 miles (485 km) across wintry northern New Mexico to a reservation on the eastern plains. Hundreds died during this tragic march, which became known as the Long Walk. The Navajos were allowed to return to their traditional homelands in 1868, after agreeing to a new peace with the United States government. Yet they were an exception in terms of keeping their homelands. Slowly, most native groups were moved from their lands. The last of the Indian wars in New Mexico ended when Geronimo and his band surrendered in 1886.

By the time the Anglos came to New Mexico in large numbers, the area's Pueblo groups and Hispanic settlers had inhabited New Mexico together for more than two hundred years. As farmers and ranchers, they had banded together for protection from the raids of other tribes. They had intermarried to some degree and had also, to some extent, learned to share and accept each other's culture. But the Anglos brought a new culture and way of life. After the Civil War, Anglos took over the territorial government and achieved positions of power in many New Mexican communities.

The New New Mexico

In the second half of the nineteenth century, the New Mexico Territory became part of the lively American West. The territory filled with cowboys, railroad workers, miners, gunfighters, gamblers, and adventurers. Cattle ranching became big business as new railroads made it easier to transport cattle to eastern markets. But the sudden growth led to conflicts. Cattle ranches needed water, and landowners argued over water rights. In Lincoln County, a feud between cattle ranchers turned into a long and bloody war. One local gunfighter, nicknamed Billy the Kid, became a legend. He was celebrated in poems, songs, and even a symphony.

As early as 1850, New Mexicans asked Congress to make New Mexico a U.S. state. But many members of Congress were unsure. Some did not trust New

Billy the Kid was twenty-one years old in 1881 when he was shot and killed by Sheriff Pat Garrett, after having been convicted of murder and escaping from jail.

Mexicans, most of whom were either Hispanic or American Indian, and did not like the fact that many New Mexicans' primary language was Spanish. So Congress did not approve statehood, and the New Mexico Territory was created instead. Distrust of New Mexicans arose again in 1898 during the Spanish-American War. Some people in the eastern United States believed that New Mexico's large Hispanic population would cause it to side with Spain in the war. President William McKinley nevertheless asked New Mexico's territorial governor to send volunteers to help the war effort. The response was overwhelming. Future president Theodore Roosevelt welcomed many New Mexican soldiers into the Rough Riders. This volunteer cavalry unit led by Roosevelt helped to free the island of Cuba from Spanish rule. Finally, on January 6, 1912, New Mexico was granted statehood, becoming the forty-seventh U.S. state.

Changes Big and Small

In the early 1900s, doctors in the East started sending patients to New Mexico for the warm weather and the clean, dry air. Artists, writers, photographers, and tourists came as well and were struck by the region's beauty. In a letter from Santa Fe, the photographer Ansel Adams wrote, "This is a place to work—and dream."

Along with the people who came for the area's healthful climate and natural beauty were those who wanted to make a living off the land. Mining companies dug for copper, silver, lead, gold, and other minerals. Energy companies drilled for oil

Copper mining became a major industry in New Mexico in the 1900s.

Navajo code talkers served with the U.S. Marines fighting on the island of New Guinea during World War II.

and natural gas. In remote areas, the U.S. military established a number of airfields, military outposts, and research laboratories.

New Mexicans have long been active in the U.S. military. When the United States entered World War I in 1917, the newly admitted state contributed troops to the U.S. forces fighting in Europe. The state offered even more troops when the United States fought in World War II from 1941 to 1945. One noteworthy unit was the Navajo code talkers, members of the U.S. Marine Corps. From 1942 to 1945, these highly trained soldiers used a code based on their native language to deliver secret messages to U.S. soldiers on the battlefields in the Pacific, fighting against Japan. The Navajo soldiers were chosen because their language is unique and difficult to translate. At the time, fewer than thirty people who were non-Navajos could speak the language. The Japanese military included skilled code-breakers, but they never broke the Navajo code.

The Trinity atomic bomb test created a cloud of dust and gas that rose to a height of 40,000 feet (12,000 m).

The Manhattan Project was another World War II military program in which New Mexico played a major part. The purpose of the project was to secretly develop the first atomic bomb. This weapon is a powerful bomb that gets its force from the energy given off from splitting atoms—the building blocks of all matter. One of the chief scientists on the project was Robert Oppenheimer, who had camped as a child in the remote mountains of northern New Mexico, near the village of Los Alamos. He suggested that the project's main laboratory should be hidden there. When it was time to test a bomb, scientists chose a remote site near Alamogordo named Trinity. In 1945, they placed the first atomic bomb on a steel tower erected in the desert. On July 16, when they exploded the bomb, it broke windows in houses as far as 120 miles (195 km) away. Weeks later, the United States dropped similar bombs on the Japanese cities of Hiroshima and Nagasaki, which led almost immediately to the end of World War II.

In the second half of the twentieth century and the beginning of the twenty-first, people continued to move to New Mexico to live, work, and enjoy the lifestyle and natural beauty. In 1950, fewer than 700,000 people lived in the state. By 1970, the number of residents had passed one million, and by 2010, more than 2 million people called New Mexico home. Some of the newer residents came to work in mining, in government laboratories, in agriculture, and in the oil and natural gas industries. Artists and retirees have also come to New Mexico in large numbers. A lifelong resident of Las Cruces has remarked, "People just trickle in on the Interstate. First they leave California, and then they find Phoenix, Scottsdale, Tucson, and here. But when they get here, they stay." After looking at New Mexico's colorful past, it is easy to understand why people fought for the right to stay, to live, and to work in this extraordinary land.

The natural beauty of New Mexico is one of the things that continues to attract new residents. Kitchen Mesa is located near the town of Abiquiu, in the northern part of the state.

Important Dates

★ **10,000–8000** BCE Prehistoric humans hunt mammoths and bison in what is now New Mexico.

★ **1–1300** CE The Ancestral Puebloans build elaborate stone and adobe structures, including those at Chaco Canyon.

★ **300–1400** The Mogollon people farm and create pottery.

★ **1500** Pueblo people are living in villages along the Rio Grande.

★ **1536** Spaniard Álvar Núñez Cabeza de Vaca may be the first European to set foot in present-day New Mexico.

★ **1598** Don Juan de Oñate establishes the first Spanish settlement in present-day New Mexico.

★ **1680** Popé leads a Pueblo Indian revolt, forcing the Spanish to leave the region.

★ **1692** The Spanish return, led by Don Diego de Vargas.

★ **1821** Mexico wins its independence from Spain, and New Mexico becomes a province of Mexico.

★ **1821** The Santa Fe Trail opens.

★ **1848** Mexico surrenders present-day New Mexico to the United States in the treaty ending the Mexican-American War.

★ **1853** The United States buys from Mexico a strip of land in what is now southern New Mexico and Arizona. The deal is known as the Gadsden Purchase.

★ **1864** Thousands of Navajos are forced to march hundreds of miles to a reservation in eastern New Mexico. Hundreds of people die during the journey, known as the Long Walk.

★ **1886** Apache leader Geronimo surrenders, ending the last Indian war in the region.

★ **1912** New Mexico becomes the forty-seventh state.

★ **1945** The first atomic bomb is exploded, at the Trinity site near Alamogordo.

★ **1948** American Indians are granted the right to vote.

★ **2011** Susana Martinez is sworn in as New Mexico's first woman governor. She is also the first Hispanic woman governor in the United States.

3

The People

New Mexican society is based largely on three cultures: American Indian, Hispanic, and Anglo. Through the centuries, these groups of very different people have sometimes disagreed. Yet over time, they have grown to share each other's customs and traditions. Today, the numbers of Asian Americans and African Americans are increasing in the state. However, African Americans represent only about 2 percent of the population, and Asian Americans a little more than 1 percent. The three primary cultures have played the largest part in shaping the state so far. But regardless of their racial, ethnic, and cultural backgrounds, New Mexicans are proud of their communities, which are rich with diversity and heritage.

The Native People

American Indians make up more than 9 percent of the population of New Mexico. Many of these people maintain close ties to their ancestral lands and traditions. The state's three

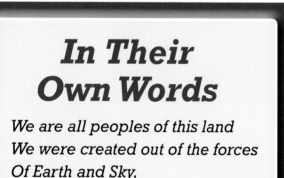

In Their Own Words

We are all peoples of this land
We were created out of the forces
Of Earth and Sky,
The stars and water. . . .

—from "The People Shall Continue"
by Simon Ortiz, Pueblo poet

The influence of Hispanic culture is evident throughout New Mexico today.

ACOMA PUEBLO

The Acoma Pueblo, located about 70 miles west of Albuquerque, is the oldest continuously inhabited community in North America. Archaeologists believe it was established in the 1100s. Nicknamed Sky City, it was built for defense, atop a 367-foot (112-m) mesa.

major American Indian groups are the Pueblo, Apache, and Navajo.

The Pueblo people share a similar culture, but they do not all speak the same native language. Of the Pueblo villages established centuries ago, nineteen remain active communities today. The people of each Pueblo village have a distinct artistic or craft tradition or means of making a living. For example, a number of people living in the Santa Clara, San Ildefonso, and Acoma pueblos are potters. Many of the Isleta Pueblo residents are farmers. Many people in the Picuris Pueblo are painters. Jewelry making is a common craft in the Santo Domingo and Zuni pueblos.

Today, not all Pueblo people live in their ancient villages. Many live in nearby towns or cities. But even for them, it is important to visit the Pueblo villages for celebrations and feast days.

The Pueblo people have been weaving blankets for centuries and using them for such practical purposes as carrying their children.

The Apache and the Navajo also add to the state's blend of native cultures. Today, many Apaches, although not all, live on reservations. The Jicarilla Apache reservation is in northern New Mexico, and the Mescalero reservation is in the south. Many Apaches work for tribal-owned ranches, resorts, and mining operations.

The Navajo Nation has 16 million acres (6.5 million hectares) in the Four Corners region. Much of the reservation lies in Arizona and Utah, but about one-third of the Navajos live in New Mexico. The town of Shiprock, New Mexico, with about 8,300 residents, is an urban center within the reservation boundaries. Navajos hold a variety of jobs, but many are weavers, silversmiths, farmers, and sheepherders. On the reservation, visitors can see Navajo hogans. These are traditional buildings that are usually round or multi-sided. They are made of logs and are sometimes covered with earth. Although only a few families in remote areas still live in hogans, many extended families, or clans, have one for special ceremonies.

Weaving beautiful rugs with geometric patterns is a traditional Navajo craft.

MAKING A ZUNI RING GAME

In the past, Zuni Pueblo children played a game using rings made from bent twigs covered with colored cord. Here is a version of the game you can play with slightly larger rings.

WHAT YOU NEED

Four jar lids, glasses, or plates of different sizes, between 2 and 6 inches (5 and 15 cm) across

Cardboard from a notepad or cereal box

Pencil

Scissors

Double-stick tape

Medium-weight yarn, 4 to 6 yards (4 to 5 m) each of blue, green, and white (traditional Zuni colors)

Cellophane tape

Place your largest lid, glass, or plate on the cardboard, trace around it, and cut out the circle. Repeat with a lid at least 2 inches (5 cm) smaller in a new spot on the cardboard. Inside each circle draw a second circle using a smaller lid. Be sure to leave a rim about $\frac{1}{2}$ inch (1 cm) wide. Cut out the inner circles, and throw those pieces away. When cutting out the inner circles, it is helpful to bend the cardboard gently to make the first cut in the middle of the circle.

Cover the two rings on both sides with pieces of double-stick tape.

Cut the yarn into 3-foot (1-m) pieces. Put one end of the white yarn through the hole in the smaller ring and wind it around and around, covering the ring completely. To finish, make a knot, cut off the extra yarn, and attach the knot to the ring with a piece of cellophane tape. Be sure to tape it down smoothly so that the ring will lie flat on the floor. Next, wind the blue and green yarn around the larger ring. Alternating the colors will create a pattern.

To play the game, place the big ring on the ground. Stand over it and try to toss the small ring so that it falls within the big one without touching it. When this gets too easy, move farther back. Figure out a scoring system and have fun.

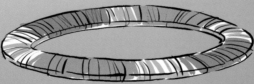

The Hispanic Tradition

Before any English colonies had been established in what is now the eastern United States, the Spanish had formed settlements in New Mexico. Spanish families in the Southwest have lived longer in the present-day United States than the descendants of the first English settlers in Virginia and New England.

In colonial times, Spanish rulers gave their nobles large land grants in Mexico and New Mexico. Landowners learned how to farm from the Pueblos and established farms as well as sheep ranches. Most of the settlers grew what they needed and traded for what they did not produce themselves. Albuquerque, founded in 1706, became an important trading center. The Spanish also first brought to New Mexico the Catholic faith, which is still practiced by many people throughout the state.

Hispanics made up most of the population of Santa Fe in the early 1800s.

RECIPE FOR GUACAMOLE

This is a simple recipe with delicious results. Guacamole has long been an important part of New Mexican cuisine. This dish is an example of how Mexican culture has helped to shape the state's foods. Have an adult help you with the cutting and chopping.

WHAT YOU NEED

2 large, ripe avocados

1 tomato, cut into small pieces

1 green onion, chopped

1 jalapeño or serrano chile pepper, seeded and chopped (wear rubber gloves to protect your hands)

$\frac{1}{4}$ teaspoon (1 gram) garlic powder

$\frac{1}{2}$ teaspoon (2 g) salt

1 $\frac{1}{2}$ teaspoons (6 g) fresh lime juice

First, peel the avocados and remove the pits. Then, using a fork, mash the avocados.

Mix the tomato, green onion, and chile pieces together.

Combine the tomato mix with the mashed avocados. Add the garlic powder and salt. Then, squeeze in the fresh lime juice. Once everything is mixed well, the guacamole is ready to serve.

It can be used as part of other Mexican dishes, such as tacos or burritos, or eaten as a dip with tortilla chips.

Today, about 46 percent of New Mexico's population is Hispanic. Some New Mexicans can trace their origins back to the noble families who were granted land by the Spanish rulers. Others are the descendants of Hispanic people who arrived later in New Mexico's history. Many of the state's new residents are immigrants from Mexico. Overall, more than 60 percent of Hispanics in New Mexico are of Mexican heritage.

Decorating buildings with lanterns called luminarias at Christmastime is a Hispanic tradition that goes back hundreds of years.

Who New Mexicans Are

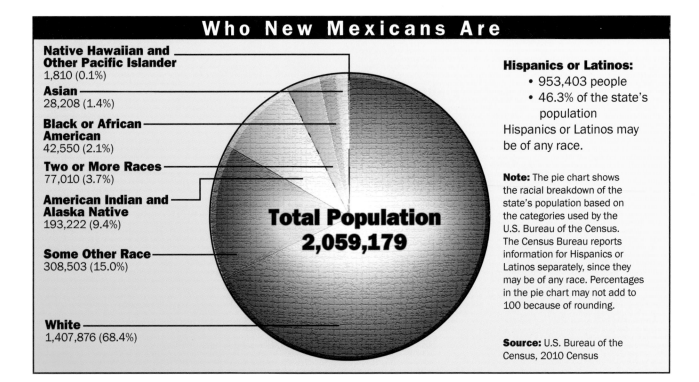

Native Hawaiian and Other Pacific Islander
1,810 (0.1%)

Asian
28,208 (1.4%)

Black or African American
42,550 (2.1%)

Two or More Races
77,010 (3.7%)

American Indian and Alaska Native
193,222 (9.4%)

Some Other Race
308,503 (15.0%)

White
1,407,876 (68.4%)

Total Population 2,059,179

Hispanics or Latinos:
- 953,403 people
- 46.3% of the state's population

Hispanics or Latinos may be of any race.

Note: The pie chart shows the racial breakdown of the state's population based on the categories used by the U.S. Bureau of the Census. The Census Bureau reports information for Hispanics or Latinos separately, since they may be of any race. Percentages in the pie chart may not add to 100 because of rounding.

Source: U.S. Bureau of the Census, 2010 Census

Through the years, New Mexican culture has been influenced deeply by Spanish traditions and language. Across the state, there are businesses, communities, and events that share and celebrate the state's Spanish heritage.

The Anglos

More than two-thirds of New Mexico's population is white. These people include descendants of the Anglos who made their way to New Mexico in the nineteenth century. Showing spirit and courage, they came as miners, cowboys, ranchers, and adventurers. Today, New Mexico's white population includes new arrivals and the descendants of many people who chose the state as their home in the twentieth century and early years of the twenty-first—drawn to the state by climate, job opportunities, or the appealing lifestyle.

Rodeos give today's cowboys a chance to show their riding skills.

Famous New Mexicans

Geronimo: Apache Leader

The given name of Apache leader Geronimo was Goyathlay, or "One Who Yawns." He was born in New Mexico in 1829. After his wife and children were killed in a Mexican army raid, he swore revenge. Reportedly, he attacked with such fury that frightened Mexican soldiers cried out to their patron saint, San Geronimo (St. Jerome), and Goyathlay took Geronimo as his warrior name. For decades, as more and more Apache land was taken over by Hispanic and Anglo settlers, he fought against the U.S. and Mexican armies, as well as raiding settlements in New Mexico, Arizona, and Mexico. He was the last American Indian leader to surrender to the U.S. government (in 1886). He died in 1909, a captive of the U.S. army in Oklahoma.

Georgia O'Keeffe: Painter

Georgia O'Keeffe was born in 1887 in Wisconsin but later moved to Ghost Ranch, New Mexico. Driving around in her Model T Ford, O'Keeffe would see a subject, stop the car, and set up her paints and easel on the side of the road. Her paintings feature desert flowers, adobe churches, and animal skeletons. She is considered one of the foremost Modernist painters in the United States. O'Keeffe died in Santa Fe in 1986.

William Hanna: Cartoonist

William Hanna was born in Melrose, New Mexico, in 1910. He loved to draw cartoons and moved to Hollywood. There, he paired up with another cartoonist, Joseph Barbera. As the team Hanna-Barbera, they were responsible for creating the cartoon characters Tom and Jerry, Huckleberry Hound, Yogi Bear and Boo-Boo, Quick Draw McGraw, Scooby Doo, the Jetsons, the Flintstones, and many more. Hanna died in California in 2001.

Nancy Lopez: Professional Golfer

Nancy Lopez was born in 1957 in California but moved to Roswell, New Mexico, when she was young. She played her first game of golf when she was eight. By the time she was twelve, she had won the New Mexico women's amateur championship. After turning professional in 1977, she won forty-eight Ladies' Professional Golf Association tournaments and became the youngest golfer ever admitted to the LPGA Hall of Fame.

Jeff Bezos: Founder of Amazon.com

Jeff Bezos was born in Albuquerque in 1964. By 1994, he was the vice president of a large financial company. Bezos, who had studied computer science in college, noticed the dramatic growth of Internet usage in the 1990s and believed that many companies were not taking advantage of the Internet's potential as a way to reach customers. So he left his job and decided to start an online bookselling business. He called his new company Amazon.com, after the huge river in South America. Today, Amazon.com is the largest online retailer in the United States. Bezos has changed the way business is done all over the world.

Neil Patrick Harris: Actor

Born in Albuquerque in 1973, Neil Patrick Harris began acting at an early age. When he was sixteen, he played the lead role in the TV series *Doogie Howser, M.D.* After the series ended in 1993, he took up stage acting and film roles. In 2005, Harris returned to television in the series *How I Met Your Mother*. He received a star on the Hollywood Walk of Fame in 2011.

Many shops in Taos sell traditional craft products to both visitors and residents.

The Arts

New Mexicans are proud that their state is nationally recognized as a center for the arts. Nature and tradition often inspire New Mexican artists. For example, the people of the Santa Clara Pueblo feel that they are part of the land. They use the same word—*nung*—to mean both people and clay. Pottery objects made in pueblos such as Cochiti, Santa Clara, Acoma, and San Ildefonso are collected by museums around the world.

American Indian jewelry makers are known for their fine work in silver and turquoise. Navajos use wool from their sheep to create highly prized rugs and blankets. The Apache are known for their elegant handmade baskets. Traditionally, New Mexico's Indians painted with sand or on rock. Today, many blend old ways with modern styles to create unique works.

In the early part of the twentieth century, Anglo artists from distant places such as New York and Europe visited Taos and Santa Fe. There, they painted the striking landscape. The best known was Georgia O'Keeffe, who observed, "All the earth colors of the painter's palette are out there in the many miles of badlands. . . ." Today, hundreds of art galleries

Quick Facts

SANTA FE, CENTER FOR THE ARTS

The United Nations Educational, Scientific, and Cultural Organization (UNESCO) has endorsed Santa Fe as a member of the Creative Cities Network. Cities worldwide belonging to this network cooperate in promoting the arts and encouraging cultural diversity. Santa Fe qualified in the Crafts and Folk Art category.

display artwork in these New Mexican cities. In Santa Fe alone, more than a dozen museums thrive.

In architecture, Spanish and Pueblo designs are combined to create what is called Santa Fe style. It features buildings constructed out of earth-colored adobe. Wood timbers, called vigas, form the framework and poke through the adobe. On the inside, an adobe fireplace is often located in the corner of the living room, and bold Navajo rugs cover clay tile floors. These buildings are both attractive and practical. The adobe and tile keep the houses cool in summer and warm in winter.

Mariachi bands include guitars and other string instruments.

Music has also been a strong part of New Mexican culture. Music lovers from around the world gather under the stars at the open-air Santa Fe Opera House to listen to classical music. American Indians use music in their ceremonies and celebrations. One well-known symbol of New Mexico is the humpbacked, flute-playing American Indian god Kokopelli, who serves his people as a magician, musician, rain priest, and song carrier. The Spanish and Mexicans brought mariachi music to the state. Anglos brought European folk songs and cowboy ballads.

Education and Sports

From kindergarten through high school, more than 325,000 students attend some 820 public schools across the state. Excellence in education has long been a priority in New Mexico. However, some rural schools suffer from inadequate financial support.

The University of New Mexico and New Mexico State University are the leading public universities in the state. The University of New Mexico's main

campus is in Albuquerque, and the State University's is in Las Cruces. Each university has four satellite campuses around the state. Other public universities include the New Mexico Institute of Mining and Technology, Eastern New Mexico University, and Western New Mexico University.

There are also several private colleges and universities in New Mexico. Included among these is St. John's College in Santa Fe, which is nationally known for its creative approach to higher education.

There are no major professional sports teams in New Mexico. But many fans root for the Lobos, the University of New Mexico teams, and the Aggies, the teams representing New Mexico State University.

Many Forms of Faith

The British novelist D. H. Lawrence said the religion of New Mexico's American Indians was "a vast old religion, greater than anything. . . ." The spiritual life of many American Indians is tied closely to nature. They celebrate their faith in kivas, in dances, and at festivals honoring the natural world. The Navajo have a ritual called the Blessing Way. A singer performs to remove evil or fear, to protect people and animals, or to ask for an agreeable life. Sometimes, a Blessing Way song can last for several days.

When the Spanish arrived and converted many of the Pueblos to Catholicism, the Indians kept many of their rituals, but they added elements of the Catholic faith. For example, traditional dances such as the Corn Dance or Deer Dance are now held on a Christian saint's day.

As Spanish priests spread their religion throughout New Mexico, they also built churches and missions that are noteworthy works of architecture. Many of these beautiful historic buildings feature adobe walls, folk paintings, elaborate carvings, and white crosses that stand out against the deep blue sky.

People of other religions have also found a home in New Mexico. Mormon temples, Protestant churches, Jewish temples, and Hindu temples contribute to the religious diversity of the state. The country's only adobe Islamic mosque is located in Abiquiu.

The San Francisco de Asis adobe church was built in the late 1700s and early 1800s.

Issues for the Future

New Mexico is not a wealthy state in terms of income (the money that is made through work). There are jobs in the cities, but not enough for everyone. In the past, many Hispanics and American Indians were farmers and ranchers. Those skills are needed less in today's economy. Today, about one in five New Mexicans lives in poverty.

In recent decades, wealthy newcomers have moved to cities such as Taos, Santa Fe, and Las Cruces to purchase or build vacation or retirement homes. Prices for land and housing in these areas went up, reaching levels many long-time residents found difficult to afford. Even though the cost of housing dropped in 2008 and subsequent years, as the whole U.S. economy went through a recession, the gap between what different groups of New Mexicans can afford has remained an issue that sometimes causes friction.

But New Mexico has a long multicultural history. New Mexicans know how to blend many ways of life to build a society that tries to represent everyone. Former U.S. congressman Steve Schiff has stated, "Despite some differences, New Mexicans on the whole deal with racial and ethnic diversity much better than the rest of the country." Jeff Bingaman, a U.S. senator from New Mexico from 1983 to 2013, thinks so too. He has affirmed, "I think most New Mexicans would agree . . . our state is a shining example of what's right."

Calendar of Events

★ Gathering of Nations Powwow

Each April in Albuquerque, more than three hundred American Indian tribes from the United States and Canada come together to share their cultures. Activities include dancing and the Indian Traders Market, which has American Indian art, artifacts, traditional foods, and other items on display and for sale.

★ Tour of the Gila Bicycle Race

In May, racers from around the world come to the high, rugged Gila Wilderness to test their mountain biking skills. Cyclists can compete in a variety of races, including some that span several days and cover hundreds of miles.

★ Clovis Pioneer Days

Every June in the eastern New Mexican city of Clovis, people enjoy parades, rodeos, quilt shows, and the Miss Rodeo New Mexico Pageant. The event celebrates the history of farming and ranching in New Mexico.

★ Roswell UFO Festival

Thousands of fans of science fiction and people interested in alien life-forms come to Roswell for its annual festival. This celebration marks the day in July 1947 when an alien spacecraft was believed by many to have crashed in a farmer's field. Roswell is home to the International UFO Museum. (UFO stands for unidentified flying object.)

★ Fiesta de Santa Fe

Late August brings the nation's oldest celebration, the Fiesta de Santa Fe. This event marks the peaceful Spanish reconquest of New Mexico after the Pueblo Revolt of 1680. The festival includes music, a crafts market, a pet parade, and the Historical/Hysterical Parade. Thousands of people watch the annual burning of Zozobra, or "Old Man Gloom." Zozobra is a 50-foot (15-m) paper puppet that symbolizes bad luck. Crowds cheer as flames make the puppet crumple. It is believed that once the puppet is burned, everyone gets a fresh start on life.

★ Hatch Chile Festival

The little town of Hatch is known as the green chile capital of the world. The number of people in town more than doubles during the chile harvest, held over Labor Day weekend. Lovers of spicy foods come to town to taste the latest chile crop.

★ New Mexico State Fair

The New Mexico State Fair is a harvest festival overflowing with ethnic foods, entertainment, arts and crafts, animal exhibits, a rodeo, concerts, and more. Held in Albuquerque each September, the fair has something for everyone.

★ Albuquerque International Balloon Fiesta

For ten days every October, one of the world's largest hot-air balloon and gas balloon events takes place. More than five hundred colorful balloons float in New Mexico's blue skies.

★ Festival of the Cranes

Each November during their migration, sandhill cranes stop at the Bosque del Apache National Wildlife Refuge, near the city of Socorro. New Mexicans celebrate the return of the cranes and other wildlife with arts and crafts, workshops, exhibits, and of course, bird-watching.

![Star with the number 4]

How the Government Works

For more than three centuries, New Mexico had governors appointed by others—Spain, Mexico, and Washington, D.C. Not until 1912, with statehood, were New Mexicans able to elect their own governor and other state government officials.

New Mexico, the State

Since New Mexico became a state, it has used the constitution that was drafted in 1911. The constitution describes the structure, the powers, and the limits on the power of state government. Many provisions in the constitution are similar to those in the U.S. Constitution, including a bill of rights. But unlike the federal Constitution, the New Mexico document includes a provision making both English and Spanish official languages.

The Palace of the Governors in Santa Fe housed governors for nearly three hundred years. Today, the state government uses a new state capitol called the Roundhouse. It is a round building designed to look like a kiva. It has four entrances that stand for the four winds, the four seasons, the four directions, and the four stages of life: infancy, youth,

Quick Facts

THE OLDEST CAPITAL CITY
Santa Fe is the oldest capital city in the nation. Founded around 1610, the city officially celebrated its 400th birthday in 2010.

New Mexico's state seal can be seen over an entrance to the capitol.

Susana Martinez won more than 60 percent of the vote in the November 2010 election to become New Mexico's first woman governor.

adulthood, and old age. The Palace of the Governors now houses the New Mexico History Museum. There are three levels of government in New Mexico: municipal, county, and state. New Mexico has thirty-three counties. People elect commissioners to run county government. Within these counties there are 104 cities, towns, or villages. These are called municipalities. People living in these areas elect councils and sometimes mayors to run their local governments. They meet with these lawmakers to discuss issues in town meetings.

The highest level is the state government. Voters elect legislators, a governor, judges, and other executive officers. Citizens also vote for people to represent them in national government. Each citizen may vote for president, two U.S. senators, and one U.S. representative. New Mexico has a total of three members in the U.S. House of Representatives. New Mexico is called a bellwether state in presidential elections. This means that New Mexican voters almost always choose the winning candidate.

New Mexico has slightly more voters belonging to the Democratic Party than to the Republican Party. About 16 percent of New Mexicans are independent voters, who have not declared membership in either major political party. National, state, and county officials tend to be a mix of both Democrats and Republicans.

Branches of Government

EXECUTIVE ★ ★ ★ ★ ★ ★ ★ ★

In the executive branch, the governor, lieutenant governor, secretary of state, and other officials are elected to four-year terms. The governor is the head of the state. His or her duties include preparing the state budget (which the state legislature must approve), suggesting new laws, and choosing cabinet members and other department heads, who carry out state laws in a certain area of responsibility, such as education or transportation. The governor also signs into law or rejects bills passed by the legislature. A governor is limited to serving two consecutive four-year terms.

LEGISLATIVE ★ ★ ★ ★ ★ ★ ★ ★

The legislative branch, or state legislature, is responsible for passing state laws. It is made up of two houses, or chambers. There is a senate, which has forty-two members, and a house of representatives, with seventy members. Each citizen can vote for one senator and one representative. Senators are elected to four-year terms, and representatives serve for two years. There is no limit on the number of terms that a member of the legislature can serve.

JUDICIAL ★ ★ ★ ★ ★ ★ ★ ★

The judicial branch is a system of courts that includes the state supreme court, the court of appeals, district courts, magistrate courts, and municipal or county courts. Magistrate, municipal, and county courts generally deal with cases involving small amounts of money, minor criminal offenses, or other criminal cases that often do not go to trial. Most criminal and other trials in major cases are held in district courts. Many district court decisions can be appealed to the court of appeals, which reviews and can change decisions. Decisions in the most serious criminal cases and certain other types of major cases can be appealed to the supreme court. The highest court in the state, the supreme court also oversees the functioning of the other courts.

Nations within a Nation

New Mexico also has tribal governments that are viewed as separate nations. Each of the nineteen pueblos, the two Apache reservations, and the Navajo Nation has an independent government. Each government includes an elected tribal council. The head of a Pueblo government is called a governor. The Apache

EXTENDING THE RIGHT TO VOTE

In 1948, all American Indians in New Mexico were allowed to vote for the first time in local, state, and federal elections. This extension of the right to vote came after a provision of the state constitution that had barred Indians from voting was struck down by a federal court on the grounds that it conflicted with the U.S. Constitution and federal law.

reservations and the Navajo Nation each elect an official called a president to head their governments. Tribal governments have their own constitutions and can collect taxes, as well as pass laws and issue regulations concerning matters ranging from hunting rules to religion. Pueblos also have an All-Indian Pueblo Council, which deals with issues affecting all the pueblos, including education and environmental concerns.

Members of the Navajo Nation tribal council have considered such issues as creating a separate Navajo Nation license plate.

Water Rights

Since New Mexico receives very little rain, access to an adequate supply of water is an important issue in the state—so important that the state constitution and state laws regulate the use of water from New Mexico's rivers, streams, and groundwater supplies (the term *groundwater* refers to natural pools of water located below the ground).

Irrigation ditches often carry water to farms and ranches in areas that receive little rain.

When New Mexico was a Spanish colony, the government granted certain people land and water rights, which their descendants or current owners of the land may still hold today. American Indian groups also have rights to water from sources that Indians have been using since ancient times. The state government recognizes these rights and tries to balance them against the needs of others. Because of the limited supply, people often have to share water sources. Groups of landowners, such as farmers and ranchers, may form associations to build, with government approval, irrigation systems, or *acequias*. The irrigation ditches take water from rivers and distribute it to people in the association. The more ditches that open onto someone's land or the closer someone's land is to the beginning of a ditch, the luckier that property owner is—since he or she will get more water. "The man who lives at the bottom of the ditch [farthest from the river that is the source of the water] is forever disappointed," one acequia manager has written.

But with so many people in need of water, problems are unavoidable. Cities such as Las Cruces, Santa Fe, Rio Rancho, and Albuquerque are growing. With more people, the cities need more water. So when local supplies run low, city governments try to obtain water from places farther away. Unfortunately, this sometimes involves using water sources that are also used by rural farming communities that rely on acequias. Farmers fear that if cities are allowed to divert too much water, there will not be enough left for the acequias. Some landowner associations have gone to court to try to prevent water diversion to cities and protect their water rights. "Water is life," is their rallying cry.

Members of the legislature met in a special session in 2011 to discuss changes to the state's voting districts.

How a Bill Becomes a Law

In New Mexico, state lawmakers introduce new bills every year to solve existing problems and make the state function better. A bill is a proposed law. Bills may be introduced by lawmakers in either the house or the senate. In a recent session, bills introduced covered such topics as water rights, training required for child care workers, and farmers' markets.

When a bill is introduced, it is given a number and read twice in the house where it was proposed. It is then assigned to one or more committees for consideration. Each committee considers bills that are related to a certain subject. For example, in the house of representatives, there is an Agriculture and Water Resources Committee.

Once in committee, a bill is discussed. At this point, public testimony is often invited, and people, companies, and organizations can give the committee their views about the bill. Committee members may make changes (amendments) to the bill. Then, they can recommend that the bill be passed, recommend that it not be passed, or send it back to the house where it originated without any recommendation.

If a committee recommends that a bill be passed, it is read a third time and then the entire house debates the bill. Amendments may be added at this time. Then, the members vote on the bill. In order for a bill to pass, it must receive a majority vote of the members present.

A bill that passes one house goes to the other house, where the same process is repeated. The second house considering the bill may make further changes to it. If the second house passes a changed version of the bill, then the bill goes to a conference committee. This committee, made up of members from both chambers, tries to resolve the differences between the two versions and work out a compromise. If it does, then a final version of the bill is sent back to both houses for their approval.

Once the two chambers have passed exactly the same version of the bill, this final bill is sent to the governor. He or she can sign the bill, in which case it becomes law. If the governor disagrees with the bill, he or she can reject, or veto, it. A vetoed bill does not become law unless both chambers of the legislature again vote in favor of it, this time by a two-thirds majority. Such an action by the legislature is called overriding the governor's veto. A governor may also take no action on a bill. In that case, the bill becomes law three days after the governor receives it, provided that the legislature is still in session. When a bill is sent to the governor less than three days before the legislature adjourns, if the governor takes no action, the bill does not become law.

Contacting Lawmakers

★ ★ ★ ★ ★ ★ ★ ★ ★ ★ ★

All citizens can contact the government officials who represent them to express their views about proposed legislation and other issues. Here are some ways you can contact New Mexico's governor, state lawmakers, and representatives in Congress.

To contact the governor, go to

http://www.governor.state.nm.us

Click on Contact the Governor under Quick Links to easily send an e-mail to the governor.

To find your state legislators, go to

http://www.nmlegis.gov/lcs/ legislatorsearch.aspx

Under Members, click on Find Your Legislator. You can search by name, district, or zip code for your representatives in both houses. If you do not know the information you need to put in, ask an adult such as a parent, teacher, or librarian to help you.

E-mail addresses, telephone numbers, and addresses for New Mexico's representatives in Congress can be found by going to this website and entering your zip code

http://www.congress.org

Making a Living

New Mexico's ancient peoples built extraordinary cities, sometimes hauling blocks of stone on their backs for long distances over rugged roads. Later, their descendants constructed elaborate irrigation systems to water their fields. Today, New Mexicans still have close ties to the land and its many gifts.

From Crafts to Technology

Manufacturing in New Mexico is different than in other states. There is no long history of factory buildings, smokestacks, or assembly lines. Instead, manufacturing is about new technologies and ancient arts.

New Mexico's economy was once based on farming and ranching. Since the 1940s, that has changed, and technology has become more and more important. During World War II, the United States needed to build up its military capability. At Los Alamos, hidden in the remote Jemez Mountains, the government set up a top-secret laboratory to develop nuclear weapons. About 300 miles (500 km) away, the first atomic bomb was tested in 1945. The test site is part of what is now called the White Sands Missile Range, which the U.S. military has used and still uses to test rockets and other advanced weapons being developed.

The government moved many scientists to New Mexico in the early 1940s, and after World War II, a number of them stayed and worked on other projects,

Chiles are an important agricultural product in New Mexico.

ROCKETS AWAY

Scientist Robert Goddard, known as the father of modern rocketry, came to New Mexico in 1930 to test new rockets he was developing. These humble beginnings led to the now-thriving aerospace industry in the state.

such as computers, robots, and energy production. Today, scientists at Los Alamos National Laboratory work on a wide range of projects, including research related to nuclear weapons, advanced computers, and renewable energy sources. Sandia National Laboratories in Albuquerque was started in 1949 as an extension of the work being done in Los Alamos. Today, scientists at Sandia focus on issues of U.S. defense and homeland security. But they also do research on climate change and on alternatives to fossil fuels.

About 50 miles (80 km) from the town of Socorro, twenty-seven dish antennas, each more than 80 feet (25 m) in diameter, form a huge Y shape. From a distance, writer Henry Shukman claimed, they seemed to be a "fleet of white sailing boats." In a way they are. But these giant dishes sail the universe

Air Force CV-22 Ospreys take off from Kirtland Air Force Base, near Albuquerque. The U.S. military is an important part of New Mexico's economy.

instead of the sea. Using radio waves instead of light waves, the dishes give scientists regular information about stars and galaxies thousands of light-years from Earth. (A light-year is the distance that something moving at the speed of light would cover in one year.) This National Science Foundation installation on the plains of New Mexico is called the Very Large Array (VLA).

The Array Operations Center in Socorro also controls a chain of ten large radio telescopes located at sites across America, extending from Hawaii to the U.S. Virgin Islands in the Caribbean Sea. These ten telescopes, including one in New Mexico, are called the Very Long Baseline Array (VLBA). The VLBA telescopes work together to provide information to astronomers about distant objects in the universe.

Technology came to New Mexico in part because of its remote and open spaces. But today, many technology products are not made in secret. The government laboratories led to the development of a "talent pool" of scientists, engineers, and other technologically skilled workers in New Mexico. Government facilities also contract out some of their activities to private companies. As a result, in recent decades dozens of private companies in the aerospace industry have located in New Mexico, employing thousands of workers to build equipment and conduct research. The skilled work force has also helped other industries start up in cities such as Albuquerque, Roswell, and Las Cruces. There, scientists and other workers make computer parts, medical devices, and pharmaceutical products. In southern New Mexico, west of the White Sands Missile Range, the state government has established Spaceport America.

Workers & Industries

Industry	Number of People Working in That Industry	Percentage of All Workers Who Are Working in That Industry
Education and health care	214,071	24.7%
Wholesale and retail businesses	121,984	14.1%
Publishing, media, entertainment, hotels, and restaurants	107,416	12.4%
Professionals, scientists, and managers	93,837	10.8%
Government	77,963	9.0%
Construction	65,003	7.5%
Manufacturing	41,001	4.7%
Other services	40,361	4.6%
Transportation and public utilities	37,624	4.3%
Banking and finance, insurance, and real estate	36,470	4.2%
Farming, fishing, forestry, and mining	32,546	3.7%
Totals	868,276	100%

Notes: Figures above do not include people in the armed forces.
"Professionals" includes people such as doctors and lawyers.
Percentages may not add to 100 because of rounding.

Source: U.S. Bureau of the Census, 2010 estimates

Handmade woven baskets have been created by craftspeople in New Mexico for hundreds of years.

Companies working with the state are hoping to make Spaceport America a major site for launching privately owned vehicles into space—in essence, an airport of the future for space travel.

Another important, though very different, form of manufacturing comes from the native peoples of the state. American Indian arts and crafts have long been an important part of New Mexico's economy. In ancient times, Indian baskets, pottery, jewelry, blankets, and other items made from woven fabrics were valuable trade goods. The same remains true today.

Tourism

Tourism is one of New Mexico's largest industries. Visitors are drawn to the state's cultural variety. The New Mexico Museum of Art in Santa Fe is the oldest museum in the state. It houses more than 20,000 works of art by Southwest artists. The Museum of International Folk Art, also in Santa Fe, is home to the world's largest collection of folk art from around the world. The Santa Fe Indian Market, held on a weekend in August each year, hosts around 100,000 visitors. Chef Mark Miller has said, "Indian Market is awash with color, sound, energy, and fragrances." On summer nights, the Santa Fe Opera House is filled with music lovers. Tourists also enjoy American Indian ceremonies and Spanish fiestas across the state. Thousands of tourists visit the multi-storied adobe buildings of the Taos Pueblo every year.

Visitors enjoy the jewelry market at the Palace of the Governors in Santa Fe.

Others visit New Mexico to see the rugged mountain ranges, deserts, canyons, and scenic rivers. They enjoy skiing, river rafting, fishing, hunting, and mountain biking. Skiers flock to Taos, Angel Fire, and the Mescalero Apache resort. In the Gila Wilderness, mountain bikers compete in international races. Another outdoor activity in New Mexico is the Albuquerque International Balloon Fiesta, where more than 500 hot-air and gas balloons take to the sky.

Champion cycler Lance Armstrong nears the finish line in the 2009 Tour of the Gila race. The race begins in Silver City, near the Gila National Forest.

Locals insist visitors to the area at the right time of year should never pass up this event.

Some of New Mexico's residents are unsure whether the tourist industry is truly good for the state. Sometimes it seems to those already there as if too many visitors decide to stay. A resident of the village of Angel Fire has commented, "Everyone who moves here wishes they were the last. . . . People here . . . are afraid it will get crowded and be nothing but traffic jams!" Some people believe that too many newcomers will harm the balance of nature. Yet others believe that income from tourism keeps a special way of life alive. Former Albuquerque mayor Martin Chavez has said, "It is economic vitality which gives us the means to preserve our natural and cultural riches, the habits of the heart."

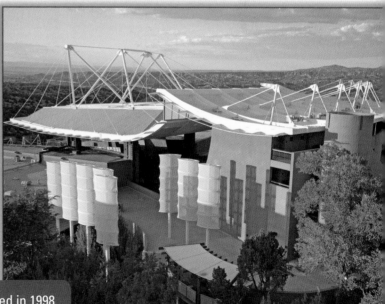

The current Santa Fe Opera House was completed in 1998.

Products & Resources

Dairy Products

The climate in New Mexico is ideal for dairy farming. New Mexico is one of the nation's top ten dairy-producing states. A Roswell cheese factory is the largest maker of mozzarella cheese in the country. It uses 4 million gallons (15 million liters) of milk a day.

Chiles

Chiles have been grown in New Mexico for at least four centuries. In recent decades, New Mexico has produced more chiles than any other state. After a harvest, people hang strands of red chiles, called *ristras*, outside to dry. The beautiful, deep-red ristras are a feast for the eyes as well as the taste buds.

Science Laboratories

In central New Mexico, many high-technology laboratories are involved in scientific research. They work in areas such as energy, pharmaceutical products, nuclear weapons, human genetics, computers, and robotics.

Copper

In 1800, an Apache warrior gave a Spanish soldier an arrow point made of copper. The soldier knew right away how important the metal was and went looking for its source. Significant amounts of copper have been mined in New Mexico ever since. The first copper taken out of New Mexico was turned into coins. Now most of the copper is used in making electrical wires and plumbing pipes.

Oil and Natural Gas

New Mexico is the tenth-ranked state in terms of total energy production. More of the state's income from mining comes from oil and natural gas than from any other source. Pipelines carry fuel to other states. New Mexico produces about one-tenth of the country's natural gas.

Tourism

Each year, more and more tourists flock to New Mexico to enjoy its scenic beauty, outdoor sports, arts and crafts, and cultural celebrations. Tourism has become one of New Mexico's largest industries.

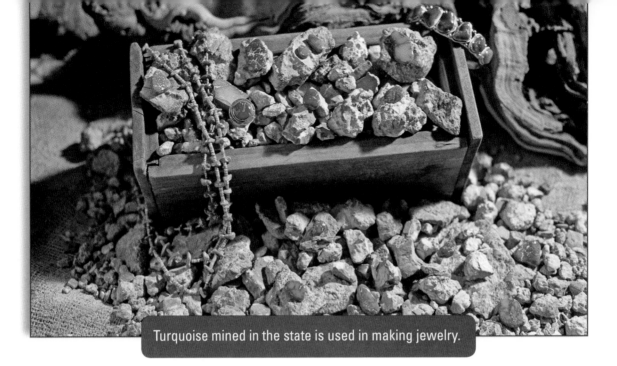

Turquoise mined in the state is used in making jewelry.

Natural Resources and Mining

In 1539, friar Marcos de Niza reported that New Mexico was "a land rich in gold, silver, and other wealth." Many Spaniards believed his words and came to the area hoping to find riches.

Mining on a significant scale did not begin until the early 1800s, however, when the Spanish started to take copper from the hills in Apache territory in the southwestern part of present-day New Mexico. They later mined gold and silver, but to this day, copper remains the state's top metal. It is used in plumbing pipes, electrical wires, and automobile parts. Mining companies have agreed to clean up their waste, but it is not always easy. One former miner has noted, "Mining here has not had so glorified a history. . . . There's no way around it, some of the things the environmentalists say are true—mining is very unsightly. Devastating. But it is controlled, and it has to be; it's a dangerous job. Our big shovels dig six dump truck loads at once."

Coal has been mined in New Mexico since the 1800s. Other minerals mined include potash, used to make fertilizer, and manganese, a metal used in making steel. New Mexico has deposits of uranium, which is a mineral that fuels nuclear power plants, nuclear submarines, and other warships. Petroleum and natural gas are also found in the state. These fuels help supply the nation's energy needs.

SMOKEY BEAR—NEW MEXICO NATIVE

Protecting the land is part of New Mexico's heritage. One famous symbol of safeguarding wilderness areas is the cartoon character Smokey Bear. The Smokey character was based on a bear cub found in New Mexico in 1950. It had been injured in a forest fire caused by careless people. The cub was rescued and lived a long life. Ever since then, in advertisements and posters, Smokey Bear has been reminding people, "Only You Can Prevent Forest Fires."

FIRE DANGER
EXTREME
TODAY
PREVENT FOREST FIRES

Living on the Land

From the earliest Mogollon farmers, farming has been a New Mexican way of life. Crops grown today include hay, corn, wheat, cotton, pecans, and chiles. In the dry northeast, farmers rely on deep wells and rainfall. One farmer's adult daughter has said, "When I visit my mom, I help her milk the cows. I don't know how she's done it all these years. Having to depend on rain, that's what makes it hard." In other dry areas, people raise cattle on long-established ranches. In the rugged northwest corner of the state, Navajos herd sheep.

Living off the land can create problems, however. For years, ranchers have argued with other concerned citizens about land and water use, as well as about the killing of wild animals. Cattle are allowed to graze on public land. But many people are opposed to this practice. They think the cattle use too much water and destroy the grasses and soil. Ranchers are concerned about losing some of their cattle to predators. They say that they have a right to protect their herds from attacks by wild animals such as wolves, coyotes, and bears. They also say elk eat crops meant for cattle. So, in cattle country, ranchers have killed off many of these animals, a practice opposed by many environmentalists.

An example of this conflict has been the controversy over the endangered Mexican gray wolf. Cattle ranchers drove away this creature a century ago. In 1998, the U.S. Forest Service reintroduced gray wolves in the Gila Wilderness. Farmers and ranchers are angry over the return of these wolves. "I can see both sides," commented one resident of the Gila Wilderness area. "I think the wolves can play a role and be a natural part of the ecosystem. But a lot of the pro-wolf people are not from here, and they don't have the roots of the locals. Still, we all get together, and we talk. The last time there was a meeting, we had to move [to a larger space], because we filled up the room."

This struggle is not the first battle over how the land is used. But time and again, New Mexicans have proved that they can find solutions that preserve their values, culture, and traditions. As the New Mexico state motto proclaims, "It grows as it goes."

State Flag & Seal

New Mexico's state flag is yellow with the state emblem, the Zia, in red. The emblem is styled after the Zia Pueblo's symbol for the sun. The rays of the sun represent central elements of the natural and spiritual worlds. The rays are four groups of four lines that stand for the four directions, the four parts of the day, the four stages of life, and the four seasons. At the center is a circle, symbolizing life.

The state seal was adopted in 1912. In the center are two eagles: the large American bald eagle and the smaller Mexican eagle. These images stand for the transfer of New Mexico from Mexico to the United States. The American eagle holds arrows in its talons, while the Mexican eagle has a snake in its beak, a reference to an ancient Aztec myth. Beneath both eagles is a scroll on which the state motto is written in Latin. The Latin words, Crescit Eundo, translate as "It grows as it goes."

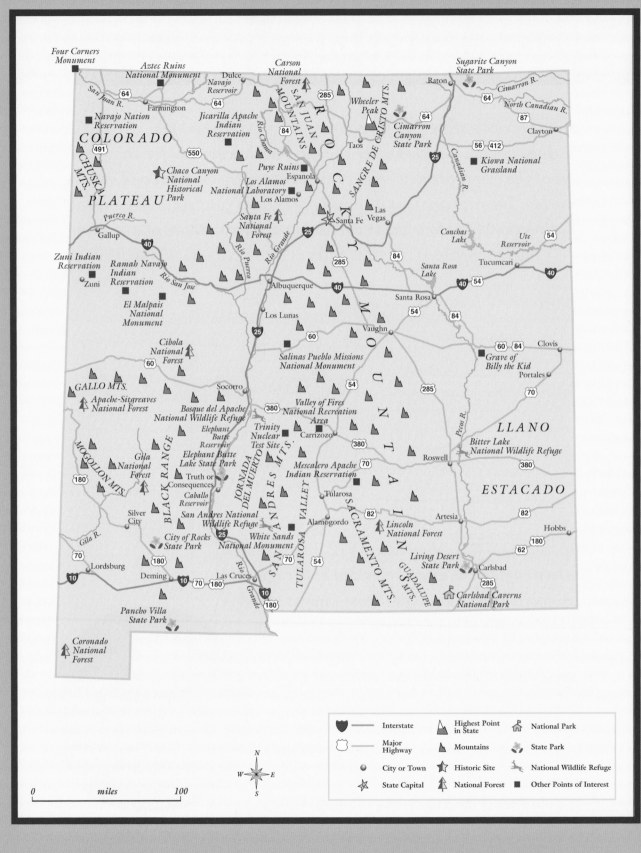

Four Corners Monument

Aztec Ruins National Monument

Sugarite Canyon State Park

Carson National Forest

64

Dulce

Navajo Reservoir

64

Farmington

285

Wheeler Peak

Raton

64

Cimarron R.

North Canadian R.

Navajo Nation Reservation

Jicarilla Apache Indian Reservation

Rio Chama

Taos

64

Cimarron Canyon State Park

Clayton

87

COLORADO

550

84

25

56 412

Kiowa National Grassland

491

Puye Ruins

CHUSKA MTS.

Chaco Canyon National Historical Park

Espanola

Las Vegas

PLATEAU

Puerco R.

Los Alamos National Laboratory

Los Alamos

Santa Fe National Forest

Conchas Lake

54

Ute Reservoir

Gallup

40

Rio Puerco

25

Santa Fe

Tucumcari

Zuni Indian Reservation

Ramah Navajo Indian Reservation

Rio San Jose

285

84

Santa Rosa Lake

40 54

40

Zuni

Albuquerque

40

Santa Rosa

El Malpais National Monument

Los Lunas

54

84

Vaughn

60 84

Clovis

Cibola National Forest

60

25

60

Salinas Pueblo Missions National Monument

Pecos R.

Grave of Billy the Kid

Portales

70

GALLO MTS.

Socorro

54

285

LLANO

Apache-Sitgreaves National Forest

Bosque del Apache National Wildlife Refuge

380

Valley of Fires National Recreation Area

Bitter Lake National Wildlife Refuge

Elephant Butte Reservoir

Trinity Nuclear Test Site

Carrizozo

MOGOLLON MTS.

Gila National Forest

Elephant Butte Lake State Park

380

Roswell

ESTACADO

380

Truth or Consequences

Mescalero Apache Indian Reservation

70

Silver City

Caballo Reservoir

Tularosa

Artesia

82

Gila R.

San Andres National Wildlife Refuge

Alamogordo

82

25

Lincoln National Forest

Hobbs

70

Lordsburg

180

City of Rocks State Park

White Sands National Monument

70 54

Living Desert State Park

62

180

10

Deming

10 70 180

Las Cruces

Carlsbad

285

Guadalupe Carlsbad Caverns National Park

10

180

Pancho Villa State Park

Coronado National Forest

	Interstate		Highest Point in State		National Park
	Major Highway		Mountains		State Park
	City or Town		Historic Site		National Wildlife Refuge
	State Capital		National Forest		Other Points of Interest

N
W E
S

0   miles   100

State Song

BOOKS

Hawkins, Aaron. *The Year Money Grew on Trees*. San Anselmo, CA: Sandpiper, 2011 (new edition).

Keegan, Marcia. *Taos Pueblo and Its Sacred Blue Lake*. Santa Fe, NM: Clear Light Publishers, 2010.

Lasky, Kathryn. *Georgia Rises: A Day in the Life of Georgia O'Keeffe*. New York: Farrar, Straus and Giroux, 2009.

Lourie, Peter. *The Lost World of the Anasazi: Exploring the Mysteries of Chaco Canyon*. Honesdale, PA: Boyds Mills Press, 2007.

Lyon, Robin. *The Spanish Missions of New Mexico*. New York: Children's Press, 2010.

Mountjoy, Shane. *Francisco Coronado and the Seven Cities of Gold*. New York: Chelsea House, 2006.

WEBSITES

Desert USA, an Exploration of North American Deserts:
http://www.desertusa.com/flora.html

Indian Pueblo Cultural Center:
http://www.indianpueblo.org

New Mexico State Government Official Website:
http://www.newmexico.gov

New Mexico Tourism Department Website for Kids:
http://www.newmexico.org/kids

Ruth Bjorklund lives on Bainbridge Island, a ferry ride away from Seattle, Washington, and two ferry rides away from Skagway, Alaska.

Ellen H. Todras is a freelance writer and editor. She has written parts of many social studies textbooks. She also has authored *Angelina Grimké: Voice of Abolition*, a young-adult biography, and other books about the United States. She loves history and enjoys bringing it to life for young people. She lives with her husband in Eugene, Oregon.

★ ★ ★ ★ ★ ★ ★ INDEX ★ ★ ★ ★ ★ ★ ★

Page numbers in **boldface** are illustrations.